MW01232638

NARCISSISTIC ABUSE

A Self Emotional Guide to Understanding
Narcissism and Healing After Hidden Psychological
and Emotional Abuse - Disarm the Narcissist and
Take Back Your Life.

By Elliott J. Power

TABLE OF CONTENTS

INTRODUCTION

C odependency is a pattern of habits and values formed when growing up by children with dysfunctional families. In order to control the family structure, these habits and values can be beneficial to the family unit because they allow it to function, and the child learns to rely on those habits. Unfortunately, these behaviors are very detrimental to the child in the long run.

Codependency is a behavior that is learned to watch our parents' acts when we are children. If our mother or father had a boundary problem, was always the martyr, could never say 'no' to people, and had dysfunctional ways to connect, we most certainly acquired these habits and carried them into our intimate relationships.

That's a lot to explain with words. First of all, what exactly is a family that is dysfunctional? In several ways, it can be defined. For this purpose, one or both parents consist of a dysfunctional family who has problems that seriously interfere with their functioning as parents and partners. Alcoholism or other drug addictions, psychiatric illnesses like depression or schizophrenia, or physical violence are some of these problems. In these painful family structures, children growing up with disabled parents acquire codependent habits and values because at least one child needs to take on some of the duties usually performed by a parent, or else the family is in complete turmoil. So a baby steps to the plate and starts to over function. The "family hero" becomes this child.

Children growing up with parents who are emotionally unavailable are at risk of being codependent, too. They find themselves in relationships where their partner is emotionally inaccessible, but they remain hopeful that the person can be changed. No matter what happens, they're not going to stop dreaming that things are going to be perfect one day.

The subconscious hope is that all the love we offer will be seen by the other person and encouraged to improve. We trust that our parents will eventually give us the love we crave if we just hang in there and share our passion, understanding, and encouragement. This thinking is dangerous if we do not have healthy boundaries that protect us from physical or emotional harm and signal to our partner that their abusive behavior is not acceptable.

The worst part is when we don't understand what's going on and continue to live in a loveless relationship because we've never learned what a good relationship looks like. Codependent individuals do not think they are deserving of love, so they settle for less. They also find themselves using their partner for mental, emotional, physical, and even sexual violence.

CHAPTER 1
THE CODEPENDENT RELATIONSHIP

W e have all heard the saying, "Relationships are about giving and taking." And it's real; it's natural to make small sacrifices when you love someone so that your partner feels valued and respected.

But what happens when one person gives too much to sacrifice his or her duties, friendships, and even identity in the relationship? That person may be engaging in what psychologists term a "codependent relationship."

Here are things you need to understand about codependent relationships:

A codependent partnership?

"One person is doing the majority of the treatment in the codependent relationship, and often ends up losing themselves in the process," Conversely, the give-and-take is relatively balanced and equitable in a stable relationship.

In a codependent relationship, there are two opposing roles that each person typically plays: the giver and the taker, says Burn. Givers tend to have a constant, subconscious need to keep their relationship alive; the fear of being alone causes them to overexert themselves physically and emotionally to please their partners, according to Burn. Takers, on the other hand, profit from this dynamic of getting a lot more than they offer. Burn states that the typical taker lacks maturity or suffers from an addiction or personality disorder.

This dynamic relationship forms a cycle that is not easy to break: According to Burn, the giver continues to overcompensate for his or her partner, while the taker avoids taking responsibility. They become co-dependent, depending not on love and treatment, but each other for relief from vulnerability.

Why do individuals get into codependent relationships?

It is essential to know the features of people predisposed to getting into them to understand how codependent relationships form. Codependent behaviors frequently date back to childhood, when we start to establish patterns of how we interact with others, or what psychologists call "attachment styles," says Dr. Holly Daniels, a clinical psychologist of Los Angeles.

A 2012 study in the American Journal of Family Therapy found that those who perceived conflict in adulthood between their parents were more likely to become co-dependent.

"The reason you build an unstable attachment style is that you didn't have stable attachments with your parents.

In codependent relationships, donors have anxious attachment types that, according to Daniels, define themselves by their relationship and will do whatever it takes to remain in it. Takers tend to have evasive attachment styles, she says, which means they want to escape emotional contact at all costs. They make exceptions, though, for anxiously attached people, because they get much more out of the relationship than they have to put in.

Givers and takers are attracted, often subconsciously, to each other. Over time, when they compete for the affirmation they can never get from the taker, givers wear themselves out. The takers, on the other hand, try to avoid their feelings and take responsibility for their actions.

How can you tell if you're in a codependent relationship?

One thing you should ask yourself is: how long on a given day do you spend thinking about your relationship? Most of the time, if the answer is, Daniels says that you are possibly codependent in your relationship.

"Also, if you seek reassurance constantly, ask questions such as, "Do you love me? "and" You promise that you will not abandon me? " you might be codependent.

Other signs of codependency include placing your partner on a pedestal, idealizing the individual despite his or her faults, and making excuses for your loved one when he or she neglects significant duties. Givers sometimes believe they're supporting their partners, when they're keeping them from personal development.

And if there is an addiction to one partner in your relationship, it's much more likely to become codependent, says Melody Beattie, author of No More Codependent. The addition of one partner to alcohol or drugs can take a toll on both partners and cause more relationship imbalances. "So can addiction to money, ego, strength, lying, or love, and sex," Beattie says. The person with the addiction will neglect his or her partner in the process, while the other may feel the need to give more to that person out of fear, remorse, or habit, according to Beattie.

It is important to take note of the signals, as codependent relationships at first will sometimes resemble healthier relationships. As time passes, givers become laden with their duties to the takers, and the giver's emotional need overwhelms the takers. Without changing course, the relationship would inevitably become miserable and unsustainable.

What do you do if you're in a codependent relationship?

I recommend obtaining clinical assistance if you have found characteristics of codependency in your relationship. Codependent connections can become more balanced and fulfilling through therapy, but both sides need to make the relationship work.

Codependent couples say that the anxiously attached partner should not let the suggestion of professional assistance be prevented by the fear of losing his or her loved one. "It is important to take the opportunity anyway." If that person is going to run away, they're going to run away anyway.

When both partners are on board, couples acknowledge their unsafe attachment styles and then advise them to "take the opposite action." For donors, that means learning to be on their own, strengthening their friendships, or focusing on passions outside of their relationship. It involves taking time for takers to initiate meaningful discussions and show more affection with their partners.

"People are not bad people in codependent relationships," says Daniels. Most individuals have some level of insecure attachment. But the secret, she says, is to learn to give, take, or walk away when it's time.

FIXING A CODEPENDENT RELATIONSHIP

For a very long period of time, I could not discern between codependency and love. I figured that if we love someone, we put that person's needs above our own and make their happiness our business.

Love is unselfish, indeed. Their needs have to come before ours when we have children. We're not going to make our baby suffer from malnutrition for hours in the middle of the night because we feel like sleeping when the baby would rather be up and feeding. When tired or would rather be doing something else, we will push our kids around to events. As a parent, behaving responsibly is part of what it means to love our children.

Nevertheless, we may be codependent when we always put the other first in our adult relationships, at the expense of our health or well-being.

About Codependency

Codependent people often look for things outside of themselves to feel better.

They shape relationships that are not safe, searching

for the other person to 'fix.' A person with codependent tendencies may be in an intimate relationship with a person who has problems with addiction that cause them to be unavailable emotionally. To avoid the sensation of emptiness in the relationship, their partner or they may be workaholics or develop some other compulsive behavior. In the short term, this is better than looking inward and coping with feelings.

How can I say if you're a codependent?

The first step to liberation, if you are in a relationship that you think might be codependent, is to avoid looking at the other and take a look at yourself.

You can be codependent if you genuinely say you agree with the following claims.

You tend to love individuals whom you can rescue and pity.

- You feel responsible for the actions of others.

- To keep the peace, you are doing more than your part in the relationship.

- You fear being abandoned or lonely.

- You feel responsible for the happiness of your partner.

- To gain your self-worth, you need approval from others.

- You have trouble adapting to change.

- You have difficulty making choices and doubt yourself often.

- You are hesitant to trust others.

- Your moods are regulated by the thoughts and feelings of those around you.

In individuals with borderline personality disorder (BPD), codependency is often seen, although this does not mean that all individuals with codependency problems also meet the criteria for a BPD diagnosis.

Relationship between addiction and codependency

One of the many concerns with a codependent relationship is that you could be unwittingly allowing the addiction of a partner. "In your effort to demonstrate your support by" helping "your partner, you may prevent him or her from getting the medication needed to get sober.

For example:

By saying he has had a stressful day or needs to relax, you justify your husband's drinking.

You make excuses when your partner can't come to social events because she is under the influence of heroin.

Whenever he complains of any minor discomfort, you let your boyfriend borrow your prescription opioids, even though you are worried about his growing drug dependence.

- You quietly take on extra responsibilities around the house or parent your children because your partner is always under the influence.

- You often find yourself apologizing to others or doing favors to repair relationships damaged by the drug or alcohol abuse of your partner.

- You risk your financial future by loaning money to your partner to cover debts incurred from substance abuse.

Addiction impairs judgment and a vital ability to think. This makes it hard for those with a drug use problem to see that they need assistance. You make it less likely that he or she would agree that a problem exists when you go out of your way to discourage your partner from witnessing the effects of drug abuse.

Loving someone with a drug use disorder may also cause your codependent tendencies to spiral out of control. If your partner is acting erratically due to drug or alcohol abuse, it is easy to revert to using codependent actions in your battle to maintain a sense of control over unpredictable environments. This creates a vicious cycle that, in a toxic and unhealthy relationship, traps both of you.

Healing from Codependency

The good news is that codependency, which means it can be unlearned, is a learned characteristic. You first and foremost need to heal yourself if you love your partner and want to sustain the relationship.

Some safe steps to restoring the relationship from

codependency include:

- Start with yourself and your partner, to be honest. Doing stuff that we don't only want to spend our time and money on, but it also creates frustration. Saying things that we do not say just harms us because we then are living a lie. Be frank in your interactions and in sharing your wishes and desires.

- Stop negative thoughts. Catch yourself when you start negative thinking. When you begin to think that you deserve to be handled poorly, catch yourself, and change your thoughts. Be constructive and have greater expectations.

- Don't take anything personally. For a codependent person, it takes a lot of work to not take things personally, particularly when in an intimate relationship. The first step is to embrace the others as they are without attempting to correct or alter them.

- Take breaks. With taking your partner for a break, there is nothing wrong. It's safe to get friendships outside of your relationship. It brings us back to our hearts to go out with friends, reminding us of who we are.

- Suggest therapy. Get into treatment with your girlfriend. A counselor acts as an independent third party. They will point out codependent patterns and behavior between the two of you that you might not be aware of. A starting point and direction can be provided by feedback. When we don't change, change can't happen.

- Depend on support from peers. Similar to Alcoholics Anonymous, Co-Dependents Anonymous is a 12-step program that assists individuals who want to break free from their patterns of codependent conduct.

- Establish limits. Those who struggle with codependency also have difficulty with boundaries. We don't know where our needs start, or where the ends of others are. We also thrive on guilt and feel guilty if we don't put the other one first.

Self-Care Is Not Selfish

When you're trying to break the cycle of codependency, it might seem like you are being driven to act in a way that is selfish and unfair to your partner. This couldn't be further from the facts.

In a stable relationship, outside of their time together, all parties have completely formed identities. Each brings distinctive characteristics to the table, establishing a relationship that allows both of them to develop and prosper.

Seeing a loved one struggling with drug or alcohol abuse is heartbreaking, but you won't be in any place to help your partner's abuse recovery unless you find time to meet your own mental health needs.

A PROFOUND LOOK INTO CODEPENDENCY SYMPTOMS

Codependency is characterized by an individual belonging to a dysfunctional, one-sided relationship. One individual relies on the other to satisfy almost all of their needs for emotional and self-esteem. It also describes a relationship that allows another individual to maintain their behavior that is irresponsible, addictive, or underachieving.

Do you spend all your energy satisfying the needs of your partner? Does your relationship make you feel trapped? Are you the one in your relationship that is continuously making sacrifices? You may then be in a codependent relationship.

For decades, the term codependency has been around. Although it was initially applied to alcoholic spouses (first called co-alcoholics), researchers showed that in the general population, the characteristics of codependents were much more prevalent than they had previously imagined. They found that if you were raised or had a sick parent in a dysfunctional family, you could also be codependent.

Researchers have also found that if left untreated, co-dependent symptoms get worse. The good news is it's reversible.

A list of codependency symptoms and being in a codependent relationship is as follows. To qualify as codependent, you don't need to have them all.

- Low self-esteem. Low self-esteem symptoms are the feeling of not being good enough or comparing yourself with others. The tricky thing about self-esteem is that some individuals think highly of themselves, but it's just a disguise; in fact, they feel unlovable or insufficient. Underneath, there are feelings of guilt, normally hidden from knowledge. Guilt and perfectionism, with low self-esteem, also go along. When all is fine, you don't feel bad about yourself.

- People-pleasing. It's OK to want someone you care about to please, but codependents don't usually believe they have a choice. "It gives them the anxiety to say" No. "Some codependents have a hard time with someone saying" No. To accommodate other people, they go out of their way and sacrifice their own needs.

- Weak boundaries. Boundaries are kind of an invisible line between you and you. It divides up what is yours and what is someone else's, which not only applies to your body, assets, and belongings, but also to your feelings, thoughts, and needs. That's where codependents get into trouble, especially. Their boundaries are blurry or weak. They feel responsible for the feelings and problems of other people or blame someone else for their own. Some co-dependents have rigid limits. They are closed off and pulled back, making it difficult for other individuals to get close to them. Sometimes, between having weak limits and having rigid ones, individuals flip back and forth.

- Reactivity. A consequence of low limits is that you respond to the thoughts and feelings of everyone. You either believe it or become defensive if someone says something that you disagree with. You absorb their words because no boundary exists. With a limit, you would realize that it was just their perspective and not a reflection of you and not feel threatened by conflicts.

- Another influence of weak boundaries is that if someone else has a problem, you want to support them to the extent that you give up yourself. To feel compassion and empathy for others is normal, but codependents begin to place others ahead of themselves. In fact, they need support and will feel rejected if another person doesn't want support. Also, even when that person does not take their advice, they keep trying to fix the other person.

- Control. The control allows codependents to feel secure and secured. In their lives, everyone needs some control over events. You wouldn't want to live in perpetual confusion and turmoil, but for codependents, regulation restricts their desire to take risks and share their feelings. Often they have an addiction that either makes them open up, like alcoholism, or lets them hold their feelings down, like workaholism, so that they don't feel out of control. Codependents also tend to regulate others close to them, since they need other people to act in a certain way to feel okay. In reality, people-pleasing and care-taking can be used to influence and exploit people. Codependents, in contrast, are bossy and tell you what you should or should not do. This is a breach of someone else's limits.

- Dysfunctional communication. Codependents have trouble communicating their ideas, emotions, and needs when it comes to it. Of course, this becomes a dilemma if you do not know what you think, feel, or need. Other times, you know, but you won't own up to your facts. You're afraid to be honest because you don't want anyone else to be upset. You could pretend that it's okay or tell someone what to do instead of saying, "I don't like that." When you are trying to manipulate the other person out of fear, communication becomes dishonest and confusing.

- Obsessions. Codependents tend to spend their time thinking about other individuals or connections. Their dependency and anxieties and fears cause this. When they feel they have made or could make a "mistake," they can also become obsessed. You can sometimes lapse into fantasy about how you would like things to be or about someone you love as a way to avoid the present pain. This a way to stay in denial discussed below, but it prevents you from living your life.

- Dependency. Codependents require other individuals to like them to feel all right about themselves. Even though they can function on their own, they're afraid of being rejected or abandoned. Others still want to be in a relationship, and when they are alone for too long, they feel sad or lonely. This characteristic makes leaving a relationship difficult for them, even though the relationship is traumatic or abusive. They end up feeling stuck.

- Denial. One of the challenges people face with having codependency assistance is that they are in denial about it, which means they are not confronting their issue. They generally think that somebody else or the situation is the problem. They either keep moaning or trying to fix the other person, or go from one relationship or job to another, never owning the reality that they have a problem. Codependents often deny their feelings and needs. Sometimes, they don't know what they feel and rely on what others think instead. For their specifications, the same thing goes. They pay heed to other people's needs and not their own. They may be in denial of their need for autonomy and space. Although some codependents seem needy, when it comes to having support, others behave like they're self-sufficient. They're not going to reach out and have trouble getting in. They are in denial of their weakness and desire for affection and love. I am not referring to sex, while sexual dysfunction is sometimes a reflection of an intimacy issue. I'm talking about being open and close with someone in an intimate relationship. You could be afraid that you would be criticized, rejected, or left, because of guilt and poor boundaries. You might, on the other hand, fear being smothered and losing your autonomy in a relationship. Your partner complains that you are unavailable. However, he or she denies his or her need for separateness. You can restrict your need for closeness and believe that your partner needs too much of your time.

Codependency induces tension and contributes to painful emotions. Shame and low self-esteem generate fear and anxiety about being judged, rejected, or abandoned; making mistakes; being a failure; feeling stuck by being near or alone. The other symptoms lead to feelings of frustration and rage, depression, hopelessness, and desperation. When there are so many emotions, you can feel numb.

For codependent individuals, there is assistance for healing and improvement. The first move is to get advice and help. These signs are deeply rooted behaviors, and on your own, they are challenging to recognize and alter. Enter a 12-step group, including Confidential Codependents, or seek therapy. Work on being more assertive and building your self-esteem.

TIPS FOR OVERCOMING CODEPENDENCE

Codependency refers to a pattern in which relationship partners or family members prioritize needs over personal needs and desires.

It goes beyond:

- Wishing to help a loved one struggling

- Feeling encouraged by their presence

- Not wanting them to quit

- Making sacrifices occasionally to help someone you love

People often use the term to define activities that don't quite match this description, contributing to some confusion. Think of it as help that becomes unhealthy, which is so severe.

In addiction therapy, the term is also used to describe encouraging behaviors in relationships impacted by drug abuse. But it can refer to any kind of partnership.

If you think you may be in a relationship that is codependent, here are some ideas to help you move forward.

First, separate showing support from codependence

Sometimes, the distinction between safe, nurturing behaviors and codependent ones can be a little fuzzy.

After all, it's normal to want to help your partner, especially if they're having a rough time.

But codependent behavior is a way to steer or monitor someone else 's behavior or mood, according to Katherine Fabrizio, a licensed clinical counselor in Raleigh, North Carolina. "You're hopping into the driver's seat of their life instead of being a passenger," she says.

It may not be your goal to monitor them, but your partner may come to rely on your assistance over time and do less for themselves. In turn, from the sacrifices you make for your partner, you might feel a sense of fulfillment or purpose.

Other key signs of codependency might include:

- Worrying about the behavior or well-being of your partner

- Worrying more than they do about the actions of your partner

- A mood that relies on how your partner is feeling or acting

In your life, recognize trends

When you've got a handle on what codependency looks like, take a step back to try to find some recurrent trends in your current and past relationships.

Ellen Biros, a licensed clinical social worker in Georgia, Suwanee, states that codependent behaviors are usually rooted in childhood. Patterns you learn from your parents and replicate in relationships generally play out again and again before you put a stop to them. But a trend is difficult to break until you realize it.

Do you have a propensity to gravitate towards individuals who require a lot of assistance? Do you have a tough time asking for support from your partner?

Codependent individuals appear to rely on affirmation from others instead of self-validation, according to Biros. These self-sacrifice tendencies could make you feel closer to your partner. You can feel aimless, insecure, or experience lower self-esteem when you're not doing stuff for them.

It is essential to simply acknowledge these patterns to overcome them.

Learn what good love looks like

Not all dysfunctional relationships are codependent, but all codependent relationships are dysfunctional in general.

This doesn't mean the codependent experiences are doomed. It's just going to take some time to get things back on track. One of the first steps in doing so is clearly to learn what looks like a good, non-codependent relationship.

"Healthy love involves a period of warmth and contentment," Biros states, "while toxic love involves a period of pain and despair."

She shares a few more signs of good love:

- Couples trust each other and themselves
- Both partners feel confident in their self-worth
- Collaborators will compromise

Your partner should care about your feelings in a healthy relationship, and you should feel comfortable expressing your emotions and needs. You should also be free to voice an opinion that varies from your partner's or says no to anything that clashes with your own needs.

Set boundaries for yourself

A boundary is a limit that you place around items in which you are not comfortable. They're not always easy to set or stick to, particularly if you're struggling with long-standing codependency. You may be so used to making others happy that you have a hard time taking your boundaries into account.

Before you can powerfully and frequently respect your limits, it could take some practice, but these tips can help:

Listen with empathy, but where you end. Don't suggest suggestions or attempt to fix them unless you're active with the problem.

Practice courteous denials. "Try," I'm sorry, but at the moment, I'm not free "or" I'd prefer not to be tonight, but maybe another day.

Question yourself. Tell yourself the following questions before you do something:

- Why do I do this?

- Do I want to, or do I feel like I must?

- Will any of my money be depleted by this?

Would I still have the energy to fulfill my requirements?

Note, you can only control your actions

Trying to monitor the actions of someone else usually doesn't work out. But if you feel justified by your ability to support and care for your partner, failing at this will make you feel pretty miserable.

Their lack of progress could make you disappointed. You may feel resentful or discouraged that there was no impact on your helpful efforts. These feelings can either leave you feeling worthless or more determined to try and start the cycle again, even harder.

How do you avoid this pattern?

Remind yourself that only you can influence you. You must control your habits and responses. You aren't responsible for your partner's actions or someone else's.

Giving up control means embracing confusion. No one knows what the future holds. This can be frightening, particularly if feelings of being alone or losing your relationship lead to codependent behaviors. But the better your relationship is, the more likely it is to last.

Offer safe support

Nothing is wrong with wanting to support your partner, but without compromising your own needs, there are ways to do so.

Good support may include:

Learning regarding topics to get new viewpoints

listening to your partner's troubles or fears

Discussing potential options for them rather than for them

Providing advice or suggestions when requested, then stepping back to let them make their own decisions

offering sympathy and acceptance

Note, you can express respect for your partner by spending time with them and being there for them without attempting to control or guide their actions. Partners, not what they do with each other, should respect each other for who they are.

Practice appreciating yourself

There are also ties between codependency and low self-esteem. If you relate your self-worth to your ability to care for others, it may prove challenging to build a sense of self-worth that does not depend on your relationships with others.

But your confidence, satisfaction, and self-esteem can be improved by improved self-worth. All of this will make it easier for you to articulate your needs and set limits, all of which are crucial to overcoming codependency.

Learning to respect yourself takes time. These tips will put you in the right direction to follow:

- Spending time with individuals who treat you well. Leaving a relationship isn't always easy, even when you're ready to move on. Meanwhile, surround yourself with supportive individuals that respect you and provide encouragement and acceptance. For people who waste your energy and say or do things that make you feel bad about yourself, restrict your time.

- Do stuff that you love. Perhaps you were discouraged from having hobbies or other interests by the time you spent looking after others. Whether it's reading a book or taking a stroll, consider setting aside some time each day to do things that make you happy. Take care of your health. Caring after your body, too, will help to improve your mental well-being. Ensure that you eat properly and get enough sleep each night. There are critical requirements that you deserve to follow.

- Let go of negative self-talk. When you judge yourself, challenge these negative thought habits and reframe them instead to affirm yourself. "For instance, instead of" I'm no good, "tell yourself," I'm doing my best.

Identify your own needs

Note, codependent patterns often begin in childhood. It could have been a long time before you started dwelling on your interests and needs.

Ask yourself, regardless of someone else's wishes, what you want from life. Want to have a relationship? A family? Unique kind of employment? To reside elsewhere? Whatever these questions pose, try journaling.

It can help to try new things. If you aren't sure what you like, try stuff that interests you. You might discover you have a talent or ability you never knew about.

This isn't a fast operation. It can take weeks, months, or even years to create clear ideas about what you need and want. But it's OK. The crucial part is that it is something you worry about.

Consider counseling

Codependent habits can become so rooted in personality and behavior that you can have a hard time finding them on your own. Codependency can be difficult to conquer solo, even though you note them.

Biros suggests finding support from a therapist who focuses on healing from this challenging condition if you're focusing on resolving codependency.

They will motivate you:

Identifying and taking action to remedy codependent conduct patterns

- work on improving self-esteem

- Exploring what you want out of life

- reframe and challenge negative thinking patterns

"Continuing to place your attention outside of yourself brings you into a position of powerlessness," Fabrizio says. Over time, this can lead to feelings of hopelessness and helplessness, which can contribute to depression.

Codependency is a complicated problem, but with a little effort, you can resolve it and start creating more healthy relationships that serve your needs, too.

What Causes Codependency?

When individuals realize that they have codependent behaviors, they sometimes question where these codependent traits originated from. Why are certain individuals in their adult relationships vulnerable to codependency? What does codependency induce? Why is it so hard to break away from relationships that are codependent?

While the answers are not the same for everybody, it starts in childhood for most individuals. This is essential because children are extremely impressionable. Young kids do not have the cognitive skills or life experiences to realize that the relationships they see and experience are not healthy; their parents are not always right; that parents are lying and manipulating and lacking the abilities to provide a safe attachment.

Children who grow up in dysfunctional families believe that they don't matter and/or are the cause of family problems.

Families with instability appear to have some of these features:

- Unpredictable and Chaotic

- Scary and unsafe

- Unsupportive

- Emotionally and/or physically neglectful

- Blaming

- Judgmental

- Overly harsh or abusive

- Manipulative

- Shaming

- Secretive

- Deny that the family has problems and refuse outside help

- Inattentive

Unrealistic children's standards (expecting children to be better or to do something beyond what is developmentally appropriate)

The children are blamed for the issues or are told there isn't a problem (which is disturbing because the children intuitively know something is wrong, but the adults never confirm this intuition). The best way for children to understand their dysfunctional families is to listen to adults' negative and skewed messages and believe that "I'm the problem."

Children then learn that they are evil, worthless, dumb, incompetent, and the source of the instability of the family. This belief system forms the origins of adult, codependent relationships.

Several things can happen when parents are unable to provide a stable, supportive, nurturing home environment:

- You are becoming a caretaker. If your parent was incapable of fulfilling the parenting role, you might have taken on the parenting role to fill in the gaps. You took care of your parents or family, paid your bills, prepared meals, and stayed up to make sure that your mother didn't fall asleep with a lit cigarette and burn down the house.

- You discover that you can be harmed by people who claim to love you. The impression of your childhood was that your family hurt you physically and/or emotionally, deserted you, lied to you, abused you, and/or took advantage of your goodness. This becomes a familiar dynamic, and in adulthood, you let friends, lovers, or family members continue to injure you.

- You become a people-pleaser. Another way you attempt to feel in charge is to keep people satisfied. You do not speak up or disagree out of fear. You give and give. This nurtures your self-worth and gives you some psychological satisfaction.

- You're grappling with restrictions. No one has designed good boundaries for you, so yours is either too bad (constantly pleasing and caring) or too rigid (closed off and unable to open up and trust others).

- You feel guilty. You probably feel bad about a lot of stuff that you haven't done. Among these things is the failure of your parents or relatives to repair them. Even if it's illogical, there's a profound longing to rescue and repair. And your failure to improve your family adds to your feelings of insufficiency.

- You're getting frightened. At times, childhood was frightening. You didn't have any idea what to expect. It went well on several days, but there were other days that you hid, worried, and cried. You continue to have sleeplessness or nightmares now, feel on edge, and are afraid of being alone.

- You feel undeserving and imperfect. You have grown up believing and/or being told that something is wrong with you. You came to accept this as a fact because, when you didn't know any other truth, it was reiterated over and over.

- People you don't like. People have consistently betrayed and hurt you. The outcome is that it is hard to get close to and trust either your partner or close friends. This is a way for you to shield yourself from potential wounds, but it is also a barrier to true intimacy and communication.

- You won't let people support you. You're not used to your needs being met or anyone taking care of you. You feel more comfortable helping to get it. You'd rather do it by yourself than be indebted or have it used against you.

- You feel alone. You thought you were the only one for a long time with a family like this or who felt like that. You felt lonely and embarrassed by the secrets you had to keep in your childhood. It's easy to see why codependents will remain in dysfunctional relationships as adults rather than alone when you combine this loneliness with feeling afraid and flawed. Being alone often feels that you are truly flawed and unwanted as a validation.

- You become excessively accountable. As a child, your family's survival or survival depended on you taking on duties that surpassed your age. To the extent that you can overwork and have trouble relaxing and having fun, you remain an extremely reliable and responsible person. You often take responsibility for other people's feelings and acts.

Controlling you become when life feels out of control and scary by trying to control individuals and situations.

If you're codependent, this may sound very familiar and perhaps bring back some memories of childhood.

You are followed into adulthood by your

childhood

You bring with you all of these relationship complexities and unresolved conflicts in your adult relationships. You repeat them because they're familiar, even though they are unsatisfactory, confusing, and terrifying. You have no idea what a good relationship is, and you have no impression that you deserve one.

Be self-compassionate

You, as a child, are stuck. You can't leave your family, so you find ways to cope. To survive, you develop strategies. A compassionate way to look at them is to think of your codependent traits as adaptive. They served you well as a child. You're an adult now who can more clearly see the roots of your codependency. Your parents have not been able to fulfill your needs. This does not mean that you are defective. Like a terrified child who has to prove his / her worth with any action, you no longer need to live your life. It's time for the cocoon to emerge and be alive. The first step is asking for help.

CHAPTER 2
SUPPORT FOR CODEPENDENT THAT ARE ENDING RELATIONSHIP

F
or codependents, breaking up and rejection is extremely hard. Breaking up triggers secret sorrow and induces irrational guilt, rage, shame, and fear. Working through the following issues will help you let go and move on.

Codependents frequently blame themselves or their partner. They have low self-esteem, and feelings of guilt are caused by every refusal. For them, partnerships are of primary importance. They worry this relationship might be their last. They haven't grieved their childhood. Memories from their childhood of loss and trauma are caused. It can help to let go and move on by working through these problems.

Blame

One of the principal signs of codependency is weak boundaries. Codependents, with their own emotions, needs, and motives, have trouble seeing others as different people. They feel responsible for the thoughts and acts of others and are guilty. This accounts for high reactivity, tension, and caretaking in codependent relationships. They view their partner's desire for a room or split up or divorce as their responsibility. And if their spouse blamed them, it still doesn't make it so. There may be situations where the addiction, violence, or infidelity of a person precipitates a breakup. Nevertheless, if you look deeper, those actions represent individual motives and are part of a larger picture of why the relationship did not function. No one is accountable for the actions of someone else. There's always an option for people to do what they do.

Rage and anger also can keep you trapped in the past. Codependents blame others for their actions because they have difficulty accepting responsibility, which may involve a failure to set limits. As a child, they may have been accused or criticized, and blame feels normal and shields them from their overdeveloped feeling of guilt.

Low Self-Esteem and Guilt

Shame is an underlying cause of codependency and results from impaired parenting. Codependents create the idea that they are in some way fundamentally flawed and that they are unlovable. When it's not supposed to be, children may perceive parental actions as denying and punishing. Even parents who profess their love can act in ways that convey you're not loved as the unique person you are.

Shame is always unconscious, but it can lead a person to love someone who can't or don't love them. In this way, a conviction in the unlovability of one becomes a prophecy of self-fulfillment working under conscious consciousness. Some codependents have a script that shames, "I'm flawed" or "I'm a loser," blaming themselves for something that goes wrong. To justify why someone else wants to end a relationship, low self-esteem, a cognitive self-evaluation contributes to self-attribution of blame and personal defects. For instance, if a man cheats, the woman always believes that it's because she's not attractive enough, rather than because her fear of intimacy is his motivation. It can help heal guilt and boost self-esteem through learning to value yourself.

Relationships are the Key

They build strategies and protections in order to feel protected and loved in the unstable and insecure family atmosphere in which co-dependents grow up. Some seek legitimacy, some withdraw, and others attempt to gain their parents' affection by adjusting to the needs of their parents. Stereotypical codependents keep trying to make relationships work – usually more challenging than their partner –to feel comfortable and okay with themselves. The solution to their inner emptiness and uncertainty becomes a close friendship.

It is not uncommon for codependents, if they have any, to lose their mates, interests, and hobbies while they are in a relationship. They concentrate all of their attention on the relationship and their loved one, which benefits neither them nor the relationship. Instead of spending time together, several couples spend their time complaining about their relationship. When it ends, they experience the loneliness of their life without a partner. The adage, "Happiness starts inside," is relevant. Recovery from codependency makes people take responsibility for their happiness. Though a relationship can contribute to your life, if you can't do it for yourself, it won't make you happy in the long run. Getting a support group of connections or 12-step meetings and stuff that gives you pleasure regardless of whether you're in a relationship is important.

Grieving the Past

Codependents find it difficult to let go because they have not let go of their parents' childhood dream of finding the perfect love. In the way they wished their parents should have, they expect to be cared for and unconditionally supported and accepted by a spouse. For such defeats and disappointments no spouse can make up. Parents aren't flawless, and their children are frustrated by those with the best intentions. Realizing and embracing this truth, not only mentally, but emotionally, is part of being an independent adult, and that typically includes depression and sometimes frustration.

The Last Chance

It can be devastating to lose someone, as codependents attach importance to a relationship to make them happy. The natural outgrowth of shame is terror. You fear when you are embarrassed that you will not be welcomed and respected. Criticism and dismissal you fear. Codependents are fearful that they are lonely and discarded because they feel that love is unworthy. They could cling to an abusive relationship in which they're emotionally abandoned all the time. These aren't logical fears. Making a life that you enjoy prepares you to live single and be in a happier relationship where you're less reliant upon the other person to make you happy.

Trauma from the Past

It's a psychological axiom that previous losses are recapitulated with each loss. As an adult, you may have had other setbacks that intensify sadness over the present one. Yet sometimes, it's abandonment losses from childhood that are being caused. Closeness was either blissful with a parent, or maybe you never had it or did not have it reliably. The intimacy of a close friendship reminds you of the familiarity with your mother or father that you once had or longed for. It is a loss either way. Codependents may have been ignored, blamed, exploited, deceived, or rejected in childhood, and these traumas get reactivated by current events. Often, for it to be cured, they unwittingly trigger circumstances reminiscent of their experience. They can even misunderstand rejection since they continue to be handled the way they were before.

Grief is part of letting go, but the preservation of friendships and life-affirming activities in the process is vital. Blame, remorse, and guilt are not helpful, but you can help sort out your emotions and realize what you feel about the end of the current relationship by working through pain from the past. Do you miss the guy, what he or she represents, or just being in a relationship?

Letting go and healing require recognition of yourself and your partner as different individuals. Typically, relationships fail when partners have individual problems with self-esteem and guilt, are ill-matched, or have needs that they cannot connect or satisfy. Shame also causes people to drive the other person away or force him out. Healing pain and setbacks and building self-esteem helps people step on in their life and take more responsibility for themselves.

What do you need to talk about co-dependent relations?

The word 'codependency' is often used lightly to describe relationships where another person is needy or dependent on him.

There is far more to this word than daily clinginess. Much more severe than this are codependent relationships. A codependent individual will plan their whole life around satisfying the other individual, or the enabler.

In its most straightforward words, a codependent relationship is when one partner wants the other partner, who, in turn, wants to be desired. The foundation of what experts refer to when they describe the "loop" of codependency is this circular relationship.

The codependent's self-esteem and self-worth can come only from sacrificing themselves for their partner, who is only too happy to receive their sacrifices.

Quick Codependency Facts:

Among friends, romantic partners, or family members, codependent relationships may be.

- The relationship often involves emotional or physical violence.

- Family members and friends of a codependent person may know that something is wrong.

- Like any mental or emotional health issue, medication, as well as the assistance of a clinician, takes time and effort.

CODEPENDENCE VS DEPENDENCY

The difference between relying on another person, which can be a positive and beneficial trait, and codependency, which is harmful, is essential to know.

Some examples that illustrate the difference are the following:

Dependent: Two people depend on each other for support and affection. Within the relationship, both find value.

Codependent: The codependent individual feels useless because they are required by — and make drastic sacrifices for — the enabler. The enabler gets satisfaction from the other person getting them every need met.

When making extreme sacrifices for their partner, the codependent is only happy. They feel that this other person must need them to have any purpose.

Dependent: Both parties prioritize their relationship and find pleasure in external interests, friends, and hobbies.

Codependent: The codependent has no personal identity, interests, or values outside of their codependent relationship.

Dependent: Both individuals can express their feelings and needs and find ways to make both of them benefit from the relationship.

Codependent: One person believes that their desires and needs are unessential and will not express them. They may have trouble remembering their own emotions or needs at all.

Codependence may be granted to one or both parties. A codependent person can ignore other essential areas of their lives to satisfy their partner. Their intense devotion to this one person can cause damage to:

- Other experiences

- Their profession

- Their daily duties

The role of the enabler is dysfunctional too. An individual who relies on a codependent does not learn how to have a fair, two-sided relationship and always depends on the compromises and neediness of another individual.

Recognize the characteristic of codependency in your partner

An individual who is codependent and only clingy or enamored with another individual may be difficult to differentiate between. But, typically, a person who is codependent will:

- Find no joy or pleasure in life outside of doing something for the other person.

- Stay in the relationship even though they are conscious that their partner does hurtful things.

- Do something to impress and fulfill their facilitator, regardless of the cost to themselves.

- Owing to their ability to always make the other person happy, they experience intense uncertainty about their relationship.

- Using all their time and energy to give everything they ask for to their partner.

- Feel bad in the relationship for thinking about yourself and won't express any personal wishes or desires.

- Ignore their values or values to do what the other person wants.

- Other people can try to talk to the codependent about their concerns. But even though some say that the individual is too dependent, it would be hard for an individual in a codependent relationship to leave the relationship.

- The codependent person would feel intense conflict about removing themselves from the enabler because their own identity is based upon sacrificing themselves for the other person.

How does a codependent relationship develop?

Codependency is a learned trait typically resulting from previous patterns of behavior and emotional difficulties. It was once believed to be the product of an alcoholic parent staying with them.

Experts now claim that a variety of conditions will result in codependency.

Damaging parental experiences

As an infant or youth, individuals who are codependent as adults also have issues with their parental relationships. They may have been told that their own needs were less, or not at all significant than the needs of their parents. In these types of families, the child may be encouraged to concentrate on the needs of the parent and never worry about himself.

Needy parents should teach their children that children are selfish or greedy if they want something for themselves. Consequently, the child begins to neglect their own needs and instead thinks more about what they can do for others.

In these cases, one of the parents may have:

- A problem with alcohol or opioid abuse

- A lack of maturity and emotional development, which contributes to their own self-centered needs

These circumstances trigger differences in emotional growth in the child, leading them to seek out codependent relationships later.

Existing with a sick or physically ill family member

Codependency can also arise from caring for a person who is chronically ill. Being in the role of caregiver, particularly at a young age, may result in a young person neglecting their own needs and developing a habit of only helping others.

A person's self-worth can develop around being needed by another individual   and receiving nothing in return.

Codependency is not developed by many individuals who live with an ill family member. In these types of family environments, it can happen, mainly if the parent or primary caretaker in the family displays the above-mentioned dysfunctional behaviors.

Abusive relatives

Psychological disorders that last years or even a whole lifetime may be caused by physical, mental, and sexual violence. Codependency is one of the many problems that may emerge from past violence.

A child or teenager who is abused can learn to repress their emotions as a defense mechanism against the pain of violence. As an adult, this learned pattern leads to thinking more about the feelings of others and not understanding their own needs.

Often a person who is abused will seek out abusive relationships later because they are only familiar with this relationship. In codependent partnerships, this often manifests.

Care

A few factors can contribute toward establishing a healthy, respectful relationship:

Individuals in codependent relationships may need to take tiny steps in the relationship toward some separation. Outside the relationship, they may need to find a hobby or activity they enjoy.

A codependent person can continue to spend time with family members or friends who are helpful.

- The enabler must decide that they are not benefiting their codependent partner by enabling them to make drastic sacrifices.

- For persons that are in codependent relationships, individual or group counseling is very useful. A specialist may assist them in discovering ways to understand and communicate their emotions that may have been hidden since childhood.

- People who have been abused will need to accept past violence and begin to experience their desires and feelings.

- Finally, in a codependent relationship, both partners must learn to understand particular behavioral patterns, such as' having to be wanted' and requiring the other individual to concentrate their lives around them.

- These measures are not easy to do, but the effort to help both sides learn how to be in a healthy, two-sided partnership is well worth doing.

CHAPTER 3

NARCISSISM AND   CODEPENDENCY

Writers often distinguish codependents and narcissists as opposites, but interestingly, while their outward actions can vary, they share several psychological characteristics. Narcissists show core codependent symptoms of guilt, denial, dominance, (unconscious) dependence, and unstable communication and boundaries, all contributing to issues with intimacy. A strong association between narcissism and codependency was shown in one study. While it is possible to identify most narcissists as codependents, the reverse is not true; most codependents are not narcissists. They do not show traditional exploitation, privilege, and lack of empathy traits.

In our self-fixed, superstar-driven society, the word narcissism gets thrown around a lot, mostly to represent someone who seems to be unreasonably narcissistic or filled with themselves. Yet, in mental words, narcissism does not indicate self-esteem, not of an authentic nature in any case. It is increasingly true to state that people with a narcissistic character problem (NPD) are infatuated with a self-admired, gaudy image. In addition, they are totally infatuated with this swelling mental self-view in view of the fact that it helps them to escape deep feelings of vulnerability or weakness. In any case, it takes a lot of effort to sustain their visions of glory, and that's where damaged perspectives and habits come in.

A pattern of selfish, pompous logic and behavior, a lack of compassion and consideration towards others, and an over-the-top requirement towards approval are part of narcissistic personality disorder. Others also view NPD people as selfish, manipulative, narrow-minded, belittling, and demanding. In each region of the life of the narcissist, this way of reasoning and behaving surfaces: from work and fellowships to family and love relations.

In general, the term narcissism is used to describe the traits of anyone, generally, anyone who is egotistical or wants recognition. A degree of healthy narcissism, all things considered, produces an even, solid character.

Then again, there is a very different narcissistic personality disorder (NPD) that needs clear requirements to be met for a conclusion. It only affects a small number of people-a greater number of males than females. Someone with NPD is pretentious (sometimes only in fantasy), needs compassion, and needs deep respect from others, as demonstrated by five of these abridged qualities, as described in "Do You Love a Narcissist?"

Dependence

Codependency is a "missing self" condition. Codependents have missing their attachment to their intrinsic self. Their thought and actions, instead, revolve around a person, material, or process. Narcissists suffer from a lack of interaction with their authentic selves as well. They're associated with their ideal self in their position. Their inner deprivation and lack relation to their real self makes them rely on others for affirmation. Consequently, to stabilize and affirm their self-esteem and fragile ego, their self-image thought and actions are other-oriented, like other codependents.

Ironically, narcissists need praise from others amid

proclaimed high self-regard, and have an insatiable desire to be praised for getting their "narcissistic supply." This makes them dependent on others' praise as an addict is on their addiction.

Shame

At the heart of codependency and addiction is guilt. In a broken household, it comes from growing up. Self-opinion inflated by narcissists is typically mistaken for self-love. Exaggerated self-flattery and arrogance, however, merely relieve implicitly, internalized shame among codependents that is normal.

In dysfunctional families, children learn multiple ways of dealing with the fear, uncertainty, guilt, and aggression they feel growing up. Despite the good intentions of parents and the lack of overt violence, internalized shame will result. Children adopt coping behaviors to feel comfortable that give rise to an ideal self. One method is to tolerate other individuals and seek their love, affection, and approval. The searching for recognition, dominance, and supremacy over others is another one. Traditional codependents protect the first party, and narcissists protect the second. To get their needs met, they seek power and control over their world. Their pursuit of prestige, superiority, and energy helps them to avoid feeling inferior, vulnerable, needy, and helpless at all costs.

These values are normal human requirements; they are compulsive and, therefore, neurotic for codependents and narcissists, however. Additionally, the further a person pursues their ideal self, the further they depart from their real self, which only increases their fear, false self, and sense of shame.

Denial

A key symptom of codependency is denial. Generally, codependents are in denial of their codependency and also their thoughts and many needs. Likewise, narcissists deny emotions, particularly those that convey vulnerability. Many would not admit, even to themselves, to feelings of inadequacy. They disown and often project onto others feel that they consider "weak," such as longing, sadness, loneliness, powerlessness, guilt, fear, and variations. Anger makes them feel strong. Defenses against underlying humiliation are anger, greed, jealousy, and disdain.

Codependents deny their needs, incredibly emotional needs, ignored or disgraced as they grow up. Some codependents behave self-sufficient and readily put others' needs first. Some co-dependents need individuals to meet their needs. Narcissists often ignore emotional needs. They won't admit that they're demanding and insecure because having needs makes them feel dependent and inferior. As needy, they project judge.

Although narcissists typically don't put other people's needs first, some are genuinely people-pleasers and can be quite compassionate. In addition to securing the attachment of those on whom they rely, since they can support individuals they consider inferior, their motive is also for praise or to feel superior or grandiose. They may feel abused by and resentful towards the individuals they support, like most codependents.

When it comes to needs for emotional closeness, mourning, support, nurturing, and secrecy, many narcissists, hide behind a mask of self-sufficiency and aloofness. Their power search prevents them from experiencing the embarrassment of feeling vulnerable,

sad, frightened, or wanting or needing anyone —
ultimately, to escape rejection and feeling shame. Only
the danger of abandonment shows how dependent they
are.

Dysfunctional Frontiers

Narcissists have unhealthy limits, like other
codependents, since theirs were not respected growing
up. They don't perceive other people as different but as
extensions of themselves. Consequently, they project
thoughts and emotions onto others and blame them for
their shortcomings and errors, all of which they can not
accept in themselves. Also, the absence of constraints
makes them thin-skinned, too emotional, and protective,
allowing them to take it all personally.

These patterns of guilt, defensiveness, reactivity, and
taking stuff personally are expressed by many
codependents. The actions and degree or direction of
feelings-differ, but there is a common underlying
mechanism. Many codependents, for instance, respond
with self-criticism, self-blame, or isolation, while others
react with someone else's hostility and criticism or
blame. Yet, both acts are responses to guilt and display

unstable limits. (Confrontation or avoidance may be an acceptable response in certain instances, but not if it is a normal, compulsive reaction.)

Dysfunctional Communication

The engagement of narcissists is unhealthy, like other codependents. They usually lack assertiveness skills. Criticism, requests, marking, and different types of verbal violence also consist of their contact. Some narcissists, on the other hand, intellectualize, obfuscate, and are indirect. Like most co-dependents, they find it difficult to describe and clearly state their feelings. While they can more readily express ideas and take positions than other codependents, they also have difficulty listening and are dogmatic and inflexible. These are indicators of unstable communication that evidence vulnerability and lack of respect for the other individual.

Control

Narcissists want power, as other co-dependents. To feel safe, control over our environment helps us—the greater our depression and confusion, the greater our need for control. What people think, say, and do is paramount to our sense of well-being and survival because we depend on others for our survival, happiness, and self-worth. With people-pleasing, lies, or coercion, we'll try to manipulate them directly or indirectly. We try to regulate them if we're scared or ashamed of our emotions, such as rage or sorrow. Other people's grief or anger will upset us, so that they must be avoided or controlled, too.

Intimacy

Finally, for narcissists and codependents, the mixture of all these behaviors makes intimacy difficult. Relationships do not flourish without clear boundaries that offer independence and dignity to partners. They need us to be independent, to have assertive communication skills, and to have self-esteem.

NARCISSISTIC RELATIONSHIPS

Countless individuals have contacted me after writing Codependency for Dummies about their unhappiness and challenges in coping with a troublesome loved one, frequently a narcissistic spouse or parent who is uncooperative, greedy, cold, and sometimes violent.

Narcissist partners feel torn between their love and pain, between staying and leaving, but they don't seem to be able to do so either. They feel neglected, uncared for, and unessential. As the critique, demands, and emotional unavailability of the narcissist increase, their confidence and self-esteem decrease. The narcissist tends to lack empathy for their feelings and desires, despite their appeals and attempts. Over time, they become profoundly hurt and disappointed that despite their requests and goes, the narcissist continues to lack regard for their feelings and needs.

When the narcissist is a parent, the emotional rejection, influence, and criticism that they experienced growing up have adversely affected their self-esteem and ability to achieve success or sustain loving, intimate relationships by the time their children enter adulthood.

What is Narcissistic Personality Disorder?

The term narcissism is widely used to describe personality characteristics in the general population, usually narcissistic or wants attention. A level of healthy narcissism produces a well-balanced, powerful personality. Narcissistic Personality Disorder (NPD) is, on the other hand, somewhat different and requires clear conditions that must be fulfilled for a diagnosis. It only affects a small number of individuals, more males than females. As mentioned here, as demonstrated by five of these summarized characteristics, someone with NPD is grandiose (sometimes only in fantasy), lacks empathy, and needs respect from others:

1. A superb sense of self-importance exaggerates successes and skills.

2. Dreams of infinite strength, achievement, brilliance, elegance, or perfect love.

3. Lacks empathy for the thoughts and needs of others.

4. Needs excessive admiration.

5. Believes he or she is outstanding and exceptional, and can only be understood by, or can interact with other rare or high-status individuals (or institutions).

6. Unique, favorable treatment or compliance with his or her preferences is unreasonably expected.

7. Exploits and makes use of others to accomplish personal ends.

8. It envies others or feels that he or she is envious of them.

9. Gets "an attitude" of arrogance or behaves that way.

The disease ranges from moderate to severe as well. But of all those narcissists, beware of the most pernicious, aggressive, and harmful, malignant narcissists. They take traits 6 and 7 to an extreme and are vindictive and malicious.

NARCISSISTS' CHILDREN

Narcissistic parents typically run the household and can do serious harm to the self-esteem and motivation of their children. Sometimes they try to live vicariously through them. These parents expect perfection and compliance and may be competitive, envious, critical, domineering, or needy. The common factor, although their personalities differ, is that their feelings and needs come first, incredibly emotional needs. As a consequence, their kids learn to adapt, to become codependent. They bear the blame for fulfilling the parent's personal needs rather than vice versa.

While their parents feel entitled, the children think unentitled and sacrifice and ignore (unless they are narcissistic, too) their feelings and needs. They do not learn to trust themselves and respect themselves and grow up disconnected from their true self. They may be motivated to prove themselves to gain their parents' approval, but find little incentive to follow their wants and goals when not externally enforced (e.g., by a partner, employer, teacher).

While they may be unaware of what was lacking in their adolescence, fear of loss and intimacy continues to permeate their adult relationships. They're afraid to make waves or mistakes and to be honest. Some become pleasers, pretending to believe what they don't and concealing what they do, accustomed to finding external affirmation. By reenacting their family drama, they feel their only alternative is to be alone or give up themselves in a relationship.

Many adult children of narcissistic parents are depressed, have unacknowledged resentment, and feelings of loneliness. They may attract an alcoholic, a narcissist, or another unavailable spouse, repeating from childhood the cycle of emotional abandonment. Healing needs recovery from codependency and overcoming the toxic stigma gained growing up in a narcissistic family.

NARCISSISTS' PARTNERS

Partners of narcissists felt disappointed that the considerate, attentive, and loving person they fell in love with disappeared as time went on. They feel invisible and lonely and long for emotional interaction. They find it difficult, to varying degrees, to express their rights, needs, and feelings and to set limits. The relationship represents the emotional abandonment and sense of entitlement they endured in childhood. They are particularly susceptible to criticism and defenseless to narcissistic bullying because their limits were not respected growing up.

When their relationship progresses, couples admit feeling less sure of themselves than they once did. Uniformly, their self-esteem and freedom gradually decrease. Some give up their studies, job, hobbies, family relations, or friends to appease their spouse. Listen to my presentation for more on narcissistic relationships.

They sometimes experience memories of the warmth and care of the person they first fell in love with, occasionally smart, imaginative, talented, happy, handsome, or handsome. They don't hesitate to say that they're committed to remaining in the relationship, if only they felt more loved and respected. Divorce is not a choice for some people. They may be co-parenting with an ex, remaining with a spouse for parenting or financial purposes, or they want to preserve family relations with a narcissistic or challenging relative. Some would like to leave, but they lack confidence.

NARCISSISTIC MALTREATMENT

Narcissists use barriers to conceal their profound and usually unconscious guilt. They defend themselves, like bullies, by violence and through wielding authority over others. Malignant narcissists are maliciously aggressive and inflict suffering without remorse, but most narcissists, because they lack empathy, do not even know that they have hurt those nearest to them. They are more interested in averting perceived risks and satisfying their needs. Consequently, they are unaware of the severe effect of their words and actions.

Incredibly, for instance, one man couldn't understand why his wife, whom he had cheated on for a long time, wasn't pleased with him because he had found pleasure with his paramour. It was only when I found out that he suddenly grasped the mistake of his thought when most women would not be happy to learn that their partner enjoyed sexuality and companionship with another woman. He was deceived. He had unintentionally pursued the blessings of his wife because his selfish mother had never embraced his girlfriends or decisions.

Any form of abuse, whether physical, sexual, financial, mental, or emotional abuse, can include narcissistic abuse. Any type of emotional abandonment, coercion, withholding, or other uncaring behavior is most often involved. Abuse can range from the silent treatment to anger, and usually involves verbal abuse, such as accusing, insulting, attacking, demanding, lying, and belittling. It may also involve emotional blackmail or passive-aggressive behavior. If you experience domestic or intimate partner abuse, read and urgently seek support from The Facts about Domestic Violence and Abusive Relationships.

The Causes

Narcissistic Personality Disorder is similar to antisocial or borderline personality disorders in that the person who suffers is often unfairly enthusiastic. The secret explanations behind each of these can be complex, and a knowledgeable therapist knows them best.

In a dysfunctional upbringing, NPD undoubtedly has its fundamental foundations, such as exceptional spoiling, high expectations, and undue attention. Or the opposite can again be the cause of misuse and neglect. NPD sufferers believe like they are horrible, disgraceful, and despised characteristically. They have been condemned by their peers who have refused to give them friendship. They experience the shame of what their personality is, and they are powerless in the world because of this basic shame. By being very controlling and strong, they attempt to keep the weakness under control. In light of the possibility that they might be dismissed, they can't bear to open up, and dismissal is devastating for them. As it is too awful to even think of considering, their embarrassment should not be addressed to the world.

Individuals with NPD also appear to work normally at work or in social settings. Actually, as business people or at the national club, they may also be deeply effective. Yet, their intimate connections continue. There are a couple of manifestations to look for here.

Treatment

Unless they're pressured by a spouse or experience an extreme blow to their reputation or self-esteem, not many narcissists join counseling. Treating a narcissist takes considerable ability, as defined in my peer-reviewed post.

However, even if the narcissist refuses to seek support or adjust, by improving your viewpoint and actions, the relationship will markedly improve.

Most therapists attempt to co-opt the distorted ego(False Self) and defenses of the narcissist. They complement the narcissist, provoking him to prove his transcendence to resolve his disease. They deliver his path to try to dispose of ineffective, stupid, and unstable habits of conduct for flawlessness, splendor, and unceasing adoration-and his neurotic inclinations.

They would like to change or fight arbitrary shortages, reasoning mistakes, and the narcissist's victim-stance by stroking the grandiosity of the narcissist. To change his actions, they contract with the narcissist. For this issue, some also go to the medical stage, crediting it to a genetic or biochemical origin and ultimately 'absolving' the narcissist from guilt and duty and freeing his mental energy to concentrate on the care.

CHAPTER 4
RED FLAGS AND BLIND SPOTS IN DATING A NARCISSISTS

Narcissists attract people because they can be charming and charismatic. Currently, one study found that after seven meetings, their likable veneer was only penetrable. I've had several clients who believed that their narcissistic spouse's courtship was perfect, and that violence only started after the wedding. With greater insight, however, these customers admitted that there were signs they had overlooked.

BLIND SPOTS WHEN A NARCISSISTS IS DATING

There are unconscious reasons for why a narcissist could be drawn to you. Here are some reasons why you do not know a narcissist:

1. Sexual desire. The greater the sexual intensity and physical attraction, the easier it is to ignore red flags. Individuals who can see auras maintain that mental and

emotional energy is obfuscated by sexual energy, and that desire is blind.

2. Seduction. Narcissists are skilled manipulators. Some can be pretty alluring and not just sexually. They might be expert listeners and communicators, or they could attract you with flattery, self-disclosure, and insecurity, just the opposite of what a narcissist would expect.

3. Idealization. Idealization Wealthy, good-looking, safe, and/or multi-talented narcissists are also very experienced. It's simple to idealize them and, particularly if you feel inferior, want to share in the benefits of their exceptionalism. People with low self-esteem are more likely to idealize others they respect, such as co-dependents. They can be drawn to conventional narcissistic traits, such as power and boldness, that they lack. The downside is that idealization encourages one to dismiss facts to the contrary.

4. Familiarity. Intimacy. If you had a narcissistic parent, being with a narcissist would sound familiar — like kin. This attraction exists below consciousness and

is often referred to as "chemistry." This attraction can improve with personal counseling so that you can quickly spot someone violent or self-centered. Instead of being drawn to a narcissist, you might also be repelled.

5. Codependency. You might be unaware of your feelings if you have low self-esteem or are codependent, which may direct you. You do not feel entitled to value your needs and desires and have them fulfilled. Many codependents tend to accommodate, and other individuals, please others, a perfect fit for a narcissist. When you want to make a good impression, this predisposition is more significant at an early date. Thus, feelings of pain and distress that signify trouble may be ignored or rationalized. When something does annoy you, you won't speak up about it and try to forget it.

RED FLAGS WHILE A NARCISSIST IS DATING

A few red flags to watch out for are below. Getting a few characteristics does not suggest that anyone is diagnosed with NPD, but they do not bode well for a satisfying relationship. Narcissistic personality disorder.

1. Self-centricity.

For narcissists, the universe revolves around them. Some individuals are just two-dimensional, meaning that narcissists can't empathize. They are in their world and see you as an extension of themselves to fulfill their needs and desires. Is he or she interested in getting to know you when you talk about your date, or are they just curious about themselves? Surprisingly, as if their listener does not exist, some people do. This is a tell-tale hint that the relationship would make you feel invisible. If in your family you felt invisible, you may take this for granted. You might probably feel validated by the attention you offer as a good listener. Beware that this trend may continue.

As described above, some narcissists are professional communicators and may appear intrigued by you, even mirror your desires to make you like them. They can be good at short-term intimacy and make you feel like a king or queen, but ultimately, they don't keep up the act. You'll discover that their purpose is to get what they want; for example, sex, but that they're not interested in getting to know anything about you, your family, problems, or successes.

Be mindful of other signs of lack of consideration: walking well ahead of you, tracking them down for a return phone call, getting late, disregarding your limits and desires, or interrupting other people's needs with conversations.

2. Arrogance.

When they don't get what they want, narcissists feel superior to other people and maybe disrespectful or violent. In their behaviors and how they speak about themselves and others, this is revealed. Is your date a fault-finder who criticizes someone, the same sex, or an ex, or accuses them? He or she could bash you one day. Remember how he or she handles waitresses, car hops, and vendors when you go out. Does he or she display respect or superiority to other individuals in certain groups, such as minorities, immigrants, or citizens with fewer resources or education?

Narcissists want to be associated with high-status

individuals and organizations. They feel that they are the best and that they want to surround themselves with the best. This is due to vulnerability. Does your date think that only their school is the best, needing the best vehicle, the best table at the best restaurant, the finest wines, and wearing expensive labels? This can impress you, but when you feel neglected or like a prop in their lives, it will depress you later.

3. Entitlement.

This attribute is a give-away. It shows how narcissists believe that they're the core of the universe. They not only feel they're exceptional and superior to others, but also that they deserve special treatment and that laws don't apply to them. Does your date fail to turn off his or her mobile phone at the movies, expect others to do favors, cut in line, steal items like tableware, airline blankets, or hotel ashtrays, or insist on special treatment from the parking attendant, restaurant maitre d', or waiter? Does he expect you to drive to his neighborhood if you're a woman? A relationship with this person would be painfully one-sided, not a two-way path. The only interest of narcissists is to get what they want and make the relationship work for them.

4. Bragging and the need for admiration.

Although narcissists like to believe that they are superior and the best, they are inherently dangerous; therefore, they require continual affirmation, praise, and gratitude. By boasting about themselves and their successes, they pursue this. They can also lie or exaggerate. People who brag want to persuade themselves of their greatness and you.

5. Power and coercion.

Narcissists have put their needs first. With flattery, belittling, or intimidation, they can manipulate you. When planning a date, their lack of empathy will show. Time and place could be a difficult negotiation or on their terms, mainly if they sense that you are interested in them. They may want to please you to win you over; however, once they've made their "catch," they want to satisfy themselves. It is the chase, not the catch, that motivates them. They will lose interest once they're triumphant and move on to the next victory before it gets too emotionally personal. If not, they'll be emotionally inaccessible and hold you at a distance, because they're afraid if you get too close, you won't like what you see.

A Few Tips

Listen to what your dates say about past relationships and themselves. Do other individuals take responsibility or accuse them? Pay attention if they confess to significant shortcomings, problems of commitment, unfaithfulness, violence, addiction, or assault. Equally substantial, note if you feel anxious or awkward, stressed, dominated, ignored, or belittled.

Find out about narcissistic relationships, why codependents are narcissists, and why codependents are attracted to them, and vice versa. You'll gain self-esteem by healing from codependency, your estimate of your worth will improve, and you'll expect to be considered, listened to, and treated well. By establishing healthy boundaries, you can express an expectation of respect by being assertive about your beliefs, emotions, needs, and wishes, rather than pleasing others. Learn about Dealing with a Narcissist.

TYPE OF NARCISSISTIC ATTACHMENT

It feels glorious to get struck by a love bomb! Our prayers tend to be answered by lavish attention and love. We find Mr. or Ms. Right, our soul mate, unaware that a narcissist was targeting us. The bomber switches colors suddenly and loses interest, and our dream comes crashing down. Rejection, especially at the height of intimacy, is unbearable. It's a painful shock to our ears. We feel duped, cheated, and discarded. We're puzzled and try to make sense of the nightmare that was once a dream. What we thought was real was, in reality, a mirage. We quest for answers, question, and blame ourselves, sometimes losing faith in ourselves and the opposite gender.

Sometimes, spouses are ghosted by their vanishing suitor, are abandoned by text, email, or a phone call. When they're rejected in person, they're bewildered by the coldness of the narcissist, who only recently expressed love and vowed an exciting future together. They can discover that they've been disposed of for a new opportunity, cheated on, or two-timed all along.

Since all of their memories are good and good, it is painful and challenging to let go of them. It takes time to acknowledge the reality of who the bomber was. Denial protects victims from the sad truth that what they imagined was not a relationship.

NARCISSISTIC SUPPLY AND ROMANTIC BOMBING

Research reveals that love bombers have low self-esteem and are mostly narcissists, but love bombers are not always narcissists, and some are non-narcissists. Narcissists feel vulnerable and hollow, creating a façade of trust and freedom. They need continuous reassurance or "narcissistic supply" from those around them, but it is never adequate to fill their loneliness or fulfill their hunger, like vampires.

Rather than confidence, they fear that they're undesirable. What others think of them determines their sense of self; they try to control what others think to feel better. Thus, love bombing is a means to seek attention, boost their ego, and fulfill self-enhancement needs for sex, power, and control. When they're depressed, have suffered a loss, or are disenchanted with their last conquest, they look for new narcissistic supplies.

Many narcissists employ seduction, indulge in game-playing, and use self-enhancement relationships. Dating is intense and is rapidly moving. The publicity can be dizzyingly thrilling to the receiver. There's always unnecessary contact, indicating the love bombers' neediness for approval, usually by text or social media, where they can exercise more power at a distance.

Idealization & Devaluation

For a narcissist, being liked or respected is not enough. It only counts when the other person, such as wealth, beauty, special skills, strength, fame, or genius, has status or highly valued qualities. Narcissists idealize prospective partners to augment their lack of self-esteem. The feeling is, "If I can earn this wonderful person's respect, then I must be deserving of it."

When truth creeps into the relationship, they realize that their partner is insufficient or fear that as expectations for emotional intimacy rise, their imperfect, hollow self will be exposed. Every slight or perceived chink in their perfect picture of their partner feels painful. As the illusion of narcissists of their ideal mate worsens, their latent guilt is gradually causing pain. They, in turn, project this onto their partner, whom they blame and devalue. For perfectionistic narcissists, this is particularly true. If their partner's luster disappears, he or she no longer offers a suitable item to improve their self-esteem. They discard their partner and search for a new source of narcissistic supply elsewhere. The partner feels drained, hurt, resentful, and lonely when relationships with narcissists endure. Over time, indifference and lack of care destroy his or her self-esteem.

Attachment Styles

Narcissists have unstable attachment types that, or any combination, are either avoidant or nervous. Individuals with unstable attachment types felt a fundamental vulnerability resulting from relationships with early caregivers. They question others' reliability to fulfill their emotional needs and base their self-esteem on others' attitudes and responses. A study showed that people with an insecure attachment style were more likely to engage in love-bombing. (Related reading: "When a Narcissist Is Also Codependent.") One study showed that people with an insecure attachment style were more likely to engage in love-bombing.

Codependent partners

The majority of codependents often have low self-esteem and risky forms of attachment and pursue relationships to affirm their worth. Their unconscious conviction is, "So I must be lovable if I am beloved."

Although some codependents can behave in ways that seem vulnerable and insecure, narcissists, like a male peacock flaunting his feathers, mask their neediness and act self-assured, in charge, arrogant, and even cocky. This show is quite convincing to vulnerable codependents. They are fascinated and drawn to the qualities that they wish they had. They, too, idealize narcissists who immerse themselves in their appreciation. Narcissists are skillful and charming communicators, skilled at making people respect and like them. Both narcissists and codependents will adapt to each other's likes and desires, but it's a technique of seduction for the narcissist; it's a way of communicating and their personality style for the welcoming codependent. (Conquering Guilt contrasts narcissistic and codependent personality styles.)

When codependents undergo love-bombing, their low self-esteem is also boosted. Unlike in their childhood, they eventually feel seen and valued. They envision a future free of their inner emptiness and loneliness with this perfect mate who will always love them. They miss or don't see gaps or possible issues in the initial process of mutual admiration.

Codependent	vs.	Healthy Love
Intense attraction - feel anxiety		Friendship begins - feel comfortable
Idealize, and ignore differences		Get to know each other
Fall in love - make commitments		Accept differences (or leave)
Get to know each other		Grow to love each other
Become disappointed		Make commitments
Cling to romantic fantasy of love		Love and acceptance deepens
Try to change partner into ideal		Learn from each other's differences
Feel resentful and unloved		Feel supported and loved

Solutions

The good news is that we can alter our type of attachment. (Related reading: "How to change your style of attachment.") Meanwhile, when dating, it's essential to go slow. Rushing intimacy doesn't rush love, only our attachment. It's an attempt to fulfill psychological and personal needs. It takes time to know someone. That is how trust and love grow in a healthy relationship. Mature daters would not use undue seduction, charm, or make promises and declarations of love prematurely. To decide if anyone is going to be a successful long-term partner, they take time to meet, because they won't want to disappoint or harm him or her.

Keep attached to your body and your emotions. In the intensity of a new romance, question whether your "excitement" isn't anxiety about rejection and uncertain hope about a rosy future. Do you feel free to set limits and be open and frank, or are you walking on eggshells? Do you cooperate with your partner to satisfy him? In other words, can you be authentic, say " no, " and express negative feelings? That typically takes time and confidence. Many codependents say, " I trust people before they give me a reason not to. "Mature adults realize that trust must be won. Love bombers lie, but it takes time to work this out.

Watch and listen to how your date treats others and

his or her ex and talks about them. Does he or she praise you, but commands, blames, or disregards others? Your date may treat you that way one day.

The idea of getting a "better half" is as controversial as it is prevalent. Having a romantic relationship in which one person is accountable for the ability of the other to fulfill their full potential implies that without a warm body sleeping next to them, people can not effectively achieve their goals. This description of the better half is a codependency recipe, where one person compromises everything for their partnership and ends up defined by it. Instead, social scientists encourage couples to aspire for reciprocal interdependence, suggesting that no one is accountable for their aims to the other, but both help the other achieve them. It's a very dizzying concept and one explanation why experts have come up with a neat-and-tidy word for it: the phenomenon of Michelangelo, in which partners do not build grandeur from nothing, but "sculpt" what's already there. And that's how a partner, no sacrifice necessary, can bring out the best in you.

Michelangelo created stone sculptures but felt it was

essential not to impose his perspective on the stone, "Fatherly tells Marisa Cohen, a professor of psychology and coach of relationships." "Your partner should not describe you to tie this to relationships, but encourage you to show yourself. One partner allows the other to become their ideal self while working together in an interdependent manner and supports them along the way.

The impact of Michelangelo derives from the psychological philosophy of interdependence, which notes that all partnerships are a reciprocal exchange of costs and benefits. According to the theory, the best relations are associated with greater gains and the worst relationships with substantial losses, and both spouses make comparable sacrifices for the other. Partnered individuals give themselves more of an advantage over single people in doing this. Research indicates that individuals who report higher levels of relationship satisfaction are more likely to achieve the objectives they set. Other studies suggest that job performance is predicted by having a conscientious partner.

While interdependence on the surface sounds a lot

like codependency, the two have vital differences. Interdependent relationships allow individual growth through equilibrium, whereas with a lack of it, codependent ones hinder it. For example, if someone wants to start a business and they're in a codependent marriage, they're likely to be too exhausted in their relationship by their spouse's demands and stress to even entertain that concept, let alone execute it. But an individual would have the support of a sacrificial spouse in a healthy, interdependent relationship to help achieve this goal, and that would be reciprocated to help them reach their potential. Essentially, interdependence is how psychologists talk about being a good teammate. Those whose team scores the most are also good at helping.

The difference between codependency and interdependence lies in the satisfaction of relationships, an affirmation of relationships, and secure attachment, says Weltfreid. In their relationships, if couples are usually happy and not afraid of the other one leaving, or not putting one foot out the door themselves, interdependence becomes more likely. It takes time to create protection in relationships, which implies that the Michelangelo phenomenon in long-term relationships might be stronger. However, since the effect is driven by variables that fluctuate, such as the satisfaction of relationships and the affirmation of partners, it takes work to maintain over time. So it's not as simple as saying that someone is made better by a good spouse. To get Michelangelo to show up, they have to reciprocate.

"Both partners can maintain their autonomy in healthy interdependent relationships while also relying on each other for care, support, and nurturing their aspirations," Weltfreid says. "The phenomenon of Michelangelo takes place when partners influence each other in the direction of their ideal self."

How to tell if and what to do about it if you're in a narcissistic relationship

It is normal to have a partner who is sometimes self-involved. Still, you are at risk of emotional manipulation and other controlling behaviors if you find yourself in a relationship with a true narcissistic partner. Many people exhibit Narcissistic characteristics, such as the need for excessive admiration, arrogance, and exaggerated self-importance, but far fewer have a narcissistic personality disorder.

There's a distinction between being a narcissist and having narcissistic characteristics, "says Woman's Day to Dr. Rachel Gingold, Ph.D., a licensed psychologist in New Jersey."

Narcissistic personality disorder (NPD) is characterized by the Diagnostic and Statistical Manual of Mental Disorders (DSM) as an individual with at least five out of nine particular narcissistic characteristics. But these behaviors do not always manifest in the same manner.

"Rachel Schechter, a licensed professional social worker in Washington, D.C." I just think of narcissism as something on a continuum, like most mental health problems, Woman's Day is telling. While only licensed healthcare practitioners may diagnose anyone with a personality disorder, if you choose to end a partnership with a spouse displaying these characteristics, below are some examples of selfish behaviors and measures you may take.

Behaviors Narcissistic

Narcissists may exhibit any or all of the following behaviors in relationships:

"They need frequent compliments and praise, and can be very critical if they feel their partner doesn't take care of them in the way they expect," Gingold says. Requiring excessive admiration.

Control all: "Narcissists always feel the need to control all," says Schechter. "They tend to feel dominant constantly to put the people around them down."

In the mirror, a selfish person is not continually looking. Rather, they ignore the desires of their partner and lack empathy.

"Rejecting responsibility:" When things don't go the way they want, they lack a sense of responsibility. It is never their fault if something doesn't go right. They blame someone else at all times,' Schechter says.

Ignoring the needs of their partner: They don't think about the happiness of their partner or remember stuff that their partner likes. They will forget the birthday of their partner but expect a big deal to be made about their birthday. There is not so much reciprocity,' explains Gingold.

Lacking empathy: "Usually, narcissists show a lack of empathy," says Schechter. It can be confusing, however, because sometimes they may have the capacity for empathy, often for their benefit. Unlike a sociopath who does not have any empathy, there may be hints of empathy. Overall, a tell-tale sign is a lack of empathy, which is a relationship that can be very difficult to navigate.

Narcissists' Charisma

Initially, a narcissist may seem like a very appealing partner. You can be quickly attracted to their abilities to be charismatic and lavish attention on you. "If they think being with you will complement them or assist them in some way, they will be incredibly charming and doting," Gingold says. With attention, they will gush on you and seemingly idealize you. That is part of how you can trick people.

It imports this content from {embed-name}. You might be able to find the same content on their website in another format, or you may be able to find more detail.

The Narcissism Underneath

Narcissists mask deep feelings of fear behind their bravado and desperate desire for publicity. "The repressed feelings of low self-esteem are behind all this," Schechter says. They have problems with being close to anyone and try to protect themselves from anyone who sees their imperfections. They need to be perfect, and, in return, you need to be perfect. Gingold agrees, adding that "the sense of self is so weak or non-existent when it comes to narcissistic personality disorder." If things don't work out the way they want, which they never do, you're the one left getting blamed. To feel like you exist in the world, there's a reliance on external feedback.

A Narcissist Breaking Up

You can proceed cautiously if you're actually in a relationship with a narcissist. Narcissists can be very tough partners, and they often don't know they have a problem. Don't expect an easy or amicable breakup if you decide to end the relationship. "I think it would be an understatement to say that breaking up with narcissism is tricky," says Schechter. If the relationship doesn't work, then ending it is a delicate process. A narcissist is never going to say anything like, 'Oh, I get it! Without me, you're better off.

Be sure to be extremely explicit when breaking up with a narcissistic partner that the relationship is over for good. Schechter says, "Be strong and straightforward that you stick to your decision." "Don't let them persuade you otherwise, or engage you in the conduct of blame games." If a decision has been made, let them know that it is final.

"By putting yourself first and knowing your worth, try and set yourself up for success for your next relationship." Be in a healthy place first before you go into a relationship, "Gingold says." I say it to my patients repeatedly: to be in a healthy relationship, and to see what is unhealthy, your sense of self needs to be intact.

Healthy Relationship Traits

It's like a plant: it needs to be nurtured, watered and put out in the sunshine. It's not just a healthy relationship. If the plant is not properly cared for, it will begin to show signs of stress ... wilting, turning yellow ... it will eventually die. The healthy relationship passes through specific phases of development and has identifiable characteristics ...